JUNKYARD
GHOST
REVIVAL

ANIS MOJGANI
BUDDY WAKEFIELD
DERRICK BROWN
ANDREA GIBSON
ROBBIE Q. TELFER
CRISTIN O'KEEFE APTOWICZ
SONYA RENEE TAYLOR

1

Junkyard Ghost Revival

Cristin O'Keefe Aptowicz, Derrick Brown, Andrea Gibson, Anis Mojgani, Sonya Renee Taylor, Robbie Q. Telfer & Buddy Wakefield

Write Bloody Publishing ©2008

1st printing.

Printed in NASHVILLE TN USA

Cover Designed by Anis Mojgani, Cole Nuckols and dsn crz

Drawings by Anis Mojgani

Interior Layout by Lea C. Deschenes

Edited by Derrick Brown

WRITEBLOODY
QUALITY AMERICAN BOOKS AND PRINTING

JUNKYARD GHOST REVIVAL

5

JUNKYARD GHOST REVIVAL

"Four things come not back: the spoken word, the sped arrow, the past life, and the neglected opportunity."

—Proverb

ANIS MOJGANI

THE ELEPHANT WOMAN

her skin is thick to touch and hangs full
filled
with
the people that have touched it

she likes to pick flowers

she knows the Latin names of them

she sings
to no one in the morning

her voice is a vase
filled with beautiful water
that if it didn't sit so still
would be trembling

her heart is a leaf

her heart is a petal

this world is a windy one

her love is a matchstick
lit
she holds her body close around it

she can tell you the names of all the bones inside your body

she practices protection

she practices the piano

touching the keys of ivory
with a longing to swallow them
and have them return to her
the parts that were taken by so many hunters

this is her day

this is a song she jumps to snatch

her throat is soft

and it curls as she sleeps

reaching for the water in the sky

the water hanging off the leaves

and the water

deep in the earth

that moves

and moves

in the dirt

IRAN

My father's homeland is desperate for God?

the veins of mother scream for one

tell me your country can do the same

one founded on the burning of bones

one that is as empty as the weeks

our eyes bones and souls are hollow

who are you

American who are you?

you have dropped your children

as fast as everyone else has

then sink into the soft skulls of round daughters

daring to claim your index finger is more valiant

than anyone else's that you point at

I could lick my tongue across your arms

and send echoes like woodpeckers through you

and you say we are desperate for God?

yes we are

for in a world that is ruled

by a country that measures its men by the length of the skirts of the
    women they fuck

are we not all?

prove to me

that your arms are as beautiful as they could be

prove to me

that you do not not wish mine to be such

I can see it in your eyes

you hate me

I hate you too

for you are as little as I am

and this god-

this holy schizm of pathos pearls bunk bread and broken oven gold

this thing we clamor to climb over

is a yellow daisy in the breeze towering over us all

we are speck

pebble dust

and fractions of water and wind

we cut out our tongues to talk

and then use the black holes our mouths become

to measure the weight of our own blood

compared to others

how holy this is

how holy

it is to bleed

THE CAMERA

The camera could erase all memories the people in front of it
shared of one another. The young man in the dark uniform
smiled at the young girl beside him. "Now I won't have to
remember the time we were in bed and I told you I still
loved you and you sighed in exasperation. And you won't
have to think of the ones before you or of the pictures you found.
And we can just ride bicycles to the park. Wipe the crumbs off
each other's cheeks and lay upon each other without worry of
sex or sleep or love or leaving." She smiled and nodded, touched his
arm.
The photographer started reading a magazine. The girl suddenly
looked perplexed.
"But remember when you taught me to whistle? And the time you
came home
to your new house and I had already decorated it for you? The basket
of stones, the hanging metal airplane? The wooden cowboy painting?
Remember when you came to christmas at my mother's and while she
and my aunt slept down the hall we loved one another in front of the TV?
How we started making out in the car in that empty bus station
parking lot?"
The photographer looked up from his article. "I remember. But remember

when you left my place only to sit in the curb around the corner bawling?
Remember the ache the empty?" "Yes," she said softly. He pulled his ear.
"Remember the birthday party you threw me? And how you were the

one girl

that finally got me on a roller coaster?" She laughed. Then stopped.

"Remember

when you came over only to end up fighting with one another and

afterwards

we lay next to one another all night like yardsticks and decided to stop

seeing

each other?" "Yes but remember how we both felt like such shit the

next day

over how unhappy we suddenly were that we decided that was silly

and got back together?" She paused. "Remember Hawaii?" He smiled.

And looked up. She brushed something from his brow. The sun crept

through the window. The photographer decided to put some coffee on.

"The winter we first met was so cold. I had no heat, no bed. You slept

next to me

on that old fold out couch, under blankets you gave to me." He paused.

And continued. "We would lay there, you would move your fingers

over my back,

sharing secrets with my skin. You thought I was sleeping. I never was.

I was always waiting for it to happen. I don't want to forget that."

He didn't want to cry in front of her, so he put his chin down. She put

her arm around him and said, "Rub my back. Pretend we are going to bed right now, and I can't fall asleep. You remember how to do that,
    right?"
He nodded and pulled her down in to the carpet of the photo studio. She hiccuped. While the two of them lay there, the photographer went to get some milk. The man moved his fingers over the back of the girl's dress, moving them across it like drunken dragonflies, slow dancing with stillness. The girl curled against him, back to belly, like a dream and a child, and fell asleep like that. The photographer
    returned,
took a sip from his cup, and turned the page. This always happened.

THE MACHINE HAD BEEN BUILT
FOR TELEPORTATION
BUT HAD NO BODIES THAT HAD BEEN BUILT
FOR TRAVEL

When you asked from your bed where I was and I was in the basement,
I had walked there from mine, my body trying to leave my body. Tired of
laying in the same room as you and still feeling alone, wishing you would
come back to me, taking me back to you, or at least to watch waves leave
the shore and with them take a ship full of heavy sheets, white as the mist.
I don't like when tears leak their way out of me. This is why I got up and
walked from my bed, trying to get away from wherever my body still was,
it waiting for something to arrive from you that perhaps never will. I feel
how I did in those months when we didn't speak, we just sat and read,
removed from one another's shadows. This was not a good thing.
I don't like how the world moves sometimes. It moves like a cat at night
cutting through the dark, not worrying of anything else. Moves like
    two sticks
that some boy nailed together and threw up into the sky just to see the
    shape
they would create when they fell back down, the quiet sound the dust
    would make
when they landed inside of it. I don't know if I miss the feel of your arms

or just their configuration. Does that matter? Is there a difference?

Probably not. You smell beautiful. And watching the way you move

even when you don't, is still all I want to see. I like the hope of you.

And as usual when hope snakes through me, my mind rambles like a path,

walking until I am weak, pulling nails from my fingers, until I won't know

how to end this poem. I don't know how to end this poem. The computer

hums. The air conditioner is on. Outside the streets of New Orleans

bleed quietly. You are in the other room. I can hear your nose breathing

but you are probably already asleep. I will soon stop writing and fall

into the mattress that lays on the floor beside yours. Come to me dreams.

Come and leave me the parts of your selves that I can write of.

The yellow ankles. The silver wrists. The arrows and the trees

and the geese talking like the gods. Perhaps in the morning,

the words will make more sense. For now, I still have yet to learn

how to move ghosts from one side of the wall to the other,

without building a door to move them through.

CHORUS

1.

this is hard business. this love I got
she is beautiful and she is tired and she can't sleep
and my love for her is the same way
make sand
make glass
make birds from skulls
make instruments that cave in on themselves when the two of you
    sleep between them
so only her ears and yours will ever hear their sweetness
make love
but young man, don't make this poetry shit
it will burn behind your eyes so hard
she will singe the tips of her fingers when she touches you
and when the flame goes
you will still see its outline
scrambling in the dark to trace it

2.

she is beautiful and tired and she cannot sleep

3.

I wish I were her sheets

a whisker on her cat

her hip bone

an extra hand God sculpted invisible

growing out from beneath her heart

gently stroking my fingers across it

thinking to myself

I can sing in front of her

I can sing in front of her

I can sing in front of her

I can sing

so loud

so ugly and so true

that while the architects tear out their eyelashes searching for songs of her

the sun hides behind its feathers in shame

that it ever tried to convince me that I could not

PLAY THAT INSTRUMENT BOY

We will fight for you
this is what the people inside say to me
they will fight for me
for this

they wave my blood like a flag
claiming it for moon men
they bury their mothers inside of my arms
visit every sunday and leave fresh flowers upon the graves
they smile
they are filled with love
so much love they have to send some of it into other worlds
this is why they bring the flowers
this is why they wave my blood like a flag

they tell me:
boy,
play the magic strings
play those magic strings
PLAY 'em
We feel like singing

BUDDY WAKEFIELD

HORSEHEAD

When I rode off into the sunset

there was no blackout

or camera behind me.

I did not recede into the distance.

I was still very much present

with what I had left behind.

My horse was thirsty

from how far I ran him.

And your God as my witness

I ran him

until I rode into town here and realized

I am not the end of a movie.

I am done playing sunsets for lonely.

My best days are the days I see clearly

so I had hoped

to come clean here perfectly

for you and the whole saloon

but there is no polish on the table tonight.

Expect rough spots then

when I show you my cards.

These hands we were dealt

may splinter.

The spades could get under your skin.

I was livin' with'm under my skin.

They were diggin' up into my film strip.

I was ridin' with'm stuck in my heart.

It is work to ride head up and holy here.

It is painters with slack in their brush,

painters all jacked up

on stampede dust

just tryin' to get it right.

I've been trying to get it right.

I've been learning here how to grow larger

than the monsters alive in my dreams

swinging a crow bar

out of my whistle

and grand pianos out of my rust.

I shot typewriter keys out of cannons I keep

aimed at the bandits alive in my trust.

There were bandits alive in my trust

come to burn down the verbs

left alone in my blood

barkin' like dogs in a combine.

My horse head sweat

like a war on a land mine

jawbone chomp at the bit

like a bear trap telegraph.

I know I look

like a bleeding dot

by now from where you stand

where there is mad dash

and such wild west

and it is raining down locomotives on a horse

who might not have a name

but who carries a trough in his chest,

empty as it may be today

from feeding bandits disguised as the Pony Express

comin' up spades and splinters.

My workhorse spittin' out hammers and ink.

There is a colony of bad fathers

who built this place

still alive in the way I was led to think

like a snake

who can shed its own crucifixion

or a midnight rider

who leaves his beast

under whip of the daylight sky.

It's why I looked like gallop cursive

when you held me under the horizon line

to magnify

every single silver screen I stole

riding high on my filthy electric whale

like a bullet through a junkyard ghost.

Ya know, I don't care to be good, Sheriff.

I care to be whole.

So read what it says in my buckles boy

Take your sunset out of my rise.

I will not send you sailing if you came here to drive

and I know you came here to drive.

That's why it reads *don't give up* on your saddle

like I wrote *won't give up* on my life

like I've been

typing my name

on a horse I drove

through the desert as sure as a river he ran

and I swear on my shadow

he wouldn't turn back

no matter how much slack I typed into his neck.

Not everyone wants to go home

to get the sunset painted back into their bones

to have the law with all that slack in its love

pretending to save me

you don't need to save me

I already did that myself

when your god as my witness

never turned up

there was a typewriter

buried alive in that horse

I rode to get out of the flood.

I'VE SEEN NEARLY EVERY CITY FROM A ROOFTOP, WITHOUT JUMPING.

If my heart really broke every time I fell from love

I'd be able to offer you confetti by now.

But hearts don't break. They bruise and get better.

You call 911 and tell them I'm having a fantastic time.

STATED

If there's anything I've come to understand

it is that I no longer need you to fuck me as hard as I hate myself.

Make love to me like you know I am better than the worst thing I ever did.

Please go slow.

I'm new to this.

I have left my body to tell you.

SELF PORTRAIT (KNIVES)

There were knives that got stuck in the words where I came from.

Too much time in the back of my words.

I pulled knives from my back and my words.

I cut trombones from the moment you slipped away.

I've been lonely for a long time now.

Watch me smile about it.

This self portrait is from that time I cried so hard

my throat locked out all the noise.

WATER GUN

You approached me like a molehill
in the hour of my mountain.
There was a shovel
tucked into the small of your crooked back
where the water guns used to go
and I didn't see you reach for it,
Squirt.

When I welcomed you in
trust came first. There was
need no need for a cavity search
so you hid an entire sandcastle deconstruction kit
behind your eyeball
to try and tunnel through me
like an ulcer
in my child side.

I don't go lookin' for snake bites
on breathing my tubes
but there you were, teeth sunk in
caught red no-handed and rattled.

Ya got rattled when I caught ya,

became irrational when I caught ya

like a balloon we filled up

then let loose.

It was easy for you to take the wind out of my sails.

All you had to do was suck.

You're clever, the way you

slit the big out of people

then pat them on the fault lines.

Remember when I would scratch your back

then you would hold up my weakness

and stab it

with the backscratcher?

Felt like a child again

the way we both let me hate myself

as hard as I possibly could.

I still look / just like you in the mirror some days,

I still / talk like you when the time's right.

It's the reason I can't key your inner car

in good conscious. You remind me

how to make a foot in my mouth

look like I'm practicing yoga.

I learn from you
with that flashy dance floor tongue
inside your slicked back mirror ball face
reflecting all the ways you would destroy yourself
if there was no one else around.

So ya strolled up
with yer head propped high
arms stretched out like an abacus
told me I could count on you.
I ended up with zero.
My fingers got bored sliding your
beads of sweat back and forth.

We've both been a sucker for your gimmick,
pawning off the short ends of raw sticks to people
who think they can buy paid dues,
selling damaged goods and calling them gifts
to folks who still risk hope for healing.
Now everyone has a reason to keep
bringing things back to you.

Too bad there's no return policy

on those revisionist history back pedals,

or your spinal tap shoes, or the used group Huggies.

I buried your homeland insecurity tissues with

the selective memory relationship trading cards,

your open-hearted surgery blindfolds

and all those conditional rubber loves you

slipped onto your un-opposable thumb

(the one with the fake diamond ringworm)

that time ya tried strapping a

double-barreled sawed-off Band-Aid

to my middle finger applicator with wings,

you tender

chicken

breast

stroke.

You built this corner around me

because I couldn't be backed into one,

then stared down the barrel of a cheap shot

and pointed it straight at my smile.

Gunning down easy targets is for beginners, Billy Kid.

There is no high noon in my heart today.

People will drink here.

We will not shoot holes in the dam.

You have no silencer to take the bang out of my redemption.

I've got redemption for a backbone.

It holds the handle on my hammer. My heart is a hammer.

It bangs on my spine will not quit my blood.

My blood is not built to rest.

It is rushing to show you the way.

It is the only instrument I came into this world

already knowing

how to string and tune up

strum and reload

whistle and fiddle harpoon it and play.

If living

is really the greatest revenge

then I want you

to have my laughter.

And if we really do get what we give

then I give up,

so that I can

get up.

You approached me like a molehill

in the hour of my mountain

walkin' like a cocky lion

struttin' straight into the mouth of a whale.

YOUNG SOULS

Last night I had the same recurring dream,
the one where I'm on an airplane
full of babies in diapers using cell phones,
reading newspapers, and playing Suduko
in the full and upright position
who all get really passive aggressive pissy with me
because I can't stop crying like a foghorn
stuck in a stabbed cow.

One of the chubbier huffier babies
plucks the pacifier from his mouth
lifts his chest to breathe deeply
under the burden of my noise
looks right at me and says, "Dude, give it a rest."

I kick the backs of seats when I don't get the life I need.
Do not block these aisles.
If I experience self-acceptance
there should be enough room to let it in
at least the size
of all the wisdom I have offered
but not yet put to practice.

AN ANGRY GHOST

Do you remember how alone you felt that time
when you threatened to run away
because you had to clean your room
so your mom helped you pack your things
then opened the front door
and handed you a scarf,
told you a scary anecdote about hitchhiking,
then she closed the front door
and shut the blinds behind you?
Remember that?

So you ran away
into the long cold winter
for about 10 minutes
to the edge of the driveway
before realizing
you have no idea
how to bake cookies or hug yourself.
Then – remember – no one acknowledged it
when you walked back into the house
except to say,

"Oh… we thought you had run away."

Remember that?

That event is responsible for my hate and my holy moments.

You can call me an angry ghost when I'm gone

but my parents will still see me as their wide-eyed wanderer

making lists and picking my scabs.

I picked the scabs from my knees

because Mom said it would leave a scar.

I love the attention.

I helped create most of these scars

WHAT DO YOU PEOPLE DO?

When I was a child
the first thing I did upon entering someone's home
was ask where they kept their toys.
If they said they did not have any toys
I'd be like,
"What the fuck?!"

THE MATH

There are twenty-one red lights on the radio towers at the end of my city.

I can see them from the end of my street.

I don't know how they work

and have only a vague idea of what they do.

They've played that lazy blinking game with me

since I was a child in the back seat of an adult road trip

to pick up and drop off step-children.

Here's the thing I wondered:

Why were they pretending to love each other?

I am 34 years old now and I want to pull math from me

like a martial art. Wanna add the fractions they taught me;

been envious of simple formulas since the day I met the color red.

Teach me your sacred geometry.

I know there is a Pythagoras in my voice,

I just keep can't remembering what he is saying.

I did not retain the kind of information necessary to stay in my body.

I retained the way I felt that time I held my breath for twenty-nine years,

not the laws of chemistry or the mechanics of engineering.

I do not yet know how to take apart an engine block

or invest in a money system so that I can buy a plane and fly away.

This is my long division.

There were heartbroken cowboys and abandoned women

who I mistook for glory on the inside of my radio.

My parents filled our car with them

tricked me into loving heartache

like lonely is a thing to strive for.

My heart was nearly beaten to death the day you left.

Subtract this.

When the radio broke I listened to mile markers

cut passed the window of our dark green Chrysler Cordoba

and thought of good hiding places in our house

where killers don't look for fat kids. I would've stabbed nicely.

But I never had to hide in our house because killers can't hear you

when you're already dieing. Takes empathy, and practice,

like calculus. You failed calculus 3 times.

My parents kept the car window cracked

so they could smoke cigarettes and numb the night time

while the night time would shove air into the back seat on me

like a holy moment burping bursts of smoke
blowing down like the smell of, "I'm quitting. I'm quitting. I quit."

I don't know if you know this but
it is only necessary to wear a seat belt while you're sitting up.
When children lay down in the back seat
no one bothers them with what might happen.
I dream too fast to get killed in a car crash. It's simple physics.
Take me away when I'm young so I don't hurt myself no more.
Take me in my sleep so no one has to watch me cry.
I know ya can't stand it when people cry.
Reminds you of problems multiplying.

You rode in nice cars with the top down
on your way to speak three language lessons.
You learned fun skills you could show off to people
like swing dance and pole vault and
how to assemble a computer with your robot head.
I want you to show me X-ray machines and hand-eye coordination
so I can learn to stop my head before it runs off the road.
Teach me how to not flinch when I throw my heart in your face.

Let me out of these blinking lights.
Get me out of this whiney car

full of poets with their sadness and the anger.

Kill an artist and his right to be heard.

Hold me open in a window on the beaches.

Hold me steady on the wealth and on the charm.

Make it my new default position.

Make my dirty education worthy

and my fundamentals playing to win.

Make my prize consistency and the power

of being thoughtless enough to ignore your stupid bleeding hearts,

to ignore families who only think of hiding places from the killers in

their house.

I hid in a Green Cordoba on the highway.

Your math swallowed me.

Ya think

maybe

you didn't *really* love him?

Ya think

maybe

you just wanted to be him?

There's not a time I look at a photograph

when some part of me isn't staring in awe

of how somebody else figured out how to do that.

Because of the inventor of the photograph

I have memorized your image when it's still.

I wish you could see what you look like when you're still here.

DERRICK BROWN

THE RETURN OF CHRIST

Trying to let go of you is like trying to spit out my teeth
before the dashboard roars into in my throat.

Something lonely in the air has over ripened the fruit.

I want her to return to me tonight
but I don't wanna do anything different in my life.
I don't want to be a fresh lure.

I just want her to be warm, here, arms full of cake,
still shaped like a broken white viola.

Maybe I'm glad she ain't here.
I could't buy her a decent steak.
Skinny Minnie, you could use it.

Some piano is being beaten to death.
That's my kinda music.
That's the night music the kids are all choking on.
I close the hatches of my boat.

It's so still here, I can't write anything but the songs of divers,

falling into something very quiet.

The more I sit here and write this poem, the more my clothes don't fit.

The more my spaghetti brains and stubborn bruises show.

I need a drink.

All booze is just a sleeping pill now,

I close my eyes. Love.

You taste like someone waving.

I try and drink away the thing in my brain

that makes me wish these lines

are really the way I feel.

Sometimes living is a swiss bliss

and sometimes it's a rot popsicle.

The difference between bad living and bad loving

is a slipped keystroke.

I can imagine people here with me.

It scares me when they speak in the creaking of aluminum masts.

I tell them I do want her to return. They ask:

Do I know how to make that happen?

Do I have the gear to make that happen?

If Christians can wait this long for their savior to return
on an unknown open ended invite of prose,
I can wait a few years for my beautiful wand
to soar from some black ship, no longer adorning the bow
in gold paint and oak,
penetrating the coastal showgirls with that harbor light.

I know this as truth,
even if I made it up
while staring at something in the water.

PATIENCE

I can not love you until you can love our beautiful waitress
in the simple way that I do.

AFTER THE BACHELOR PARTY

Twenty seven floors up in the Hilton, Las Vegas. Almost night.

Alone and clothed in bed.

I ain't drunk anymore.

I got enough money for a sandwich tomorrow, one slot pull
and a banana.

Room 2721. The sun has dusted the mountainside.

The city is in the shadow of the wide-eyed approach of the rust bucket
  sunset.

This town is the sound of falling change, the goofy mess of noise.

Show up with shoes and bail like a baby. This is the city you run to and
  then crawl away from.

What a harlot… with her glowing brass knuckles and sympathy strokes.

I like to stand around the chrome gloom, that dumpy old sadness
sitting on every stool

all across this town with a big gulp cup full of nickles, running down
  the clock.

Drinking the classics, forgetting to eat.

Blowing your government money.

I am no longer against it.

I have fallen in love

with the choke and chance in this place.

Just having at least one chance feels good.

That's why Southern people marry young.

Who will inherit this palace of more and less and less? Not me. Not
    Hunter.

I love and I love letting go and this ain't the place for it. Either.

You show up. You drink. You wish your best friend a great honeymoon.

You go home broke and unsure why people even have bachelor parties.

I love low television after a hot shower. I love the news.

I love watching it so long,

you can hear the anchors struggle to rephrase the same story.

Someone was shot and the local station was there first.

The news got there quick and told me all about it.

I wish they could've got there beforehand.

This afternoon, it was three boys. Executed by a spirit.

My hair is wet after singing songs I hate in the shower

and my feet are sunburnt from

reading 'For Whom The Bell Tolls' by the pool

and the sheets are cool

and three boys are dead.

No one saw anything.
Bummer to die in the poverty sticks where gunshots explode
in a way that no one can hear them.
Better to die in the noise, in front of the people.

I put on my shoes to see if that makes me want to go somewhere.
It sometimes works.
I feel like there are little heaters in my shoes. I like the sunburn.

In the distance to my left,
the Stratosphere hotel is dangling people over the ledge for coaster thrills.
I get the same feeling watching casino drunks kiss. I think I'll head
    down there.

I am writing this all down because sometimes I am a believer but a
    forgetter
and sometimes I look at all the things around me that make want to
    kill all those beliefs
and say fuck it, today I am going to nowhere. I am marrying a feeling.
Today I'm selling all this shit.
Today I'm gonna call the bomb squad and ask them to dismantle me.

Today I'm gonna talk about everything I am supposed to be ashamed
to talk about.

Today I'm gonna beat off to the Song of Solomon.

Today I'm gonna throw this wine bottle into river with a blank piece
of paper inside that says 'your turn.'

Today I'm gonna pour some money I shouldn't be spending into a machine
that helps me get rid of all this future ash.

Today I'm gonna knock on your door and grab your ass and drag you
out to sea with me forever.

Today I drive with my love around my ankles and I'm gonna let you steer.

I am thrashing. Yep. Today there is an audience for me.

Tomorrow. There will be none.

A hot shower. Three boys gone. A banana.

This is living.

The sound of a casino everywhere.

You do not have to die inside.

ALL DISTORTION, ALL THE TIME

Someone plug my lungs back into the guitar amps!
I want to live on
All distortion, all the time.

Aren't you sick of being appraised as just wholesale?
Aren't you sick of sailing on listing ships?
Aren't you weary from playing cellos with ex-lover's bones?

I want the butterfly brigade to grant me a year with no stomach drama.
I want a piano that will not warp outdoors
when the rain demands slow dancing.

I want to skew the difference between Tai Chi and Chai tea,
and end up drinking a tall glass of your graceful force.

I want to lick my hands after I touch someone that has just become
razzle dazzled by tomorrows oncoming lightning.

I want birds to come close enough to hear them speak Aviation Spanish.
"Abierto! Abierto!"

I want your record collection in my throat,

and my thumb in the electric ass of the all night jukebox.

I want my shoulder blades mounted in the museum of the most

fantastic knives.

I want church in every a bar and a bar in every church.

I want to pass out and hear you say Amen in that bar.

I want a skeleton night light in the closet. Come out!

I want your wow in my now so we become NWOW.

I want the light in your attic to shine down to where my sidewalk ends.

I want free shit to not cost anything. That'd be nice.'

I want you to feel like a disco ball of fish hooks

so you can hang on my words and I can spin in your small miracles of

light.

I want my kitchen to be a Brazilian dance floor

with a pot of your sweat in the oven

and a fridge stocked with butt lust.

I want your silver muscles cut into a quilt.
Let me sleep under your strength.

I want more pony lamps. No reason.

I want to sing this feeling into all tail pipes
until I'm exhausted.

I want to smell the everything.

I want to remember that the sky is so gorgeously large,
I feel stranded beneath it.
When I gasp beneath it,
I only want to gasp for more.

YOU ARE THE OPERA

Some singers write songs
and struggle in a spinning Laundromat combat
wadding up the night
hunting for something to sing about.

Your holy ghost is a song
that's been clawing it's way out for years.
I hear your melody tonight, it is a loud one
brighter
than nightmare lightning.

Let the room look at you,
dressed up like a short story,
easy on the eyes and punchy.

You kiss like a runway virgin
and stroll like a whore outta money.
You are as soft as a wet mint
and how you soothed me like a new air conditioner.

You are not just the light,

you're the end of the tunnel.

You are the opera.

No one can rewrite you.

ANDREA GIBSON

HOW IT ENDS

It has been one year, eleven months, and six days

since the first time I saw you naked.

Since the night you ripped off your shirt,

stuck your boobs in my face and said, "Touch them."

I touched them like a diabetic third grader opening a Snickers Bar.

You said, "Hard."

I thought, "Yes, I am." But you are so soft.

I said, "Your lips are like whale blubber."

That wasn't my best line.

But it worked.

Today in the grocery store

I found one of your hairs in my underwear.

I pulled it out in the frozen food section

and screamed, "That is so gorgeous it could kill a man!"

Good thing I'm a leprechaun.

Lucky, lucky, lucky.

Baby, I have no idea how this will end.

Maybe the equator will fall like a hoola hoop from the earth's hips

and our mouths will freeze mid-kiss on our fiftieth anniversary.

Or maybe tomorrow my absolute insanity

combined with the absolute obstacle course of your communication skills

will leave us like a love letter in landfill.

But whatever, whenever, however this ends

Heather, I want you to know that right now, in this moment,

I love you forever.

I love you for the hardest mile we walked together.

For the night I collected every sharp knife in the house

and threw them one by one on the roof,

then told the sun, "Listen, show off,

for now on you are to only give me blades of grass,

things that are growing and soft,

cause there's this girl who says she wants

to float on her back through my bloodstream,

and when she does I want my rivers to reach the sea."

Do you hear me, love?

Do you know the night you told me you have a crush on my ears

I swore to never become Vangough?

And look! They're both still there!

Just like my firefly heart is still right there in your glass jar.

I've never trusted anybody more to poke enough holes in the lid.

So on the nights you sleep like a ballerina

I try to snore like a piccolo,

And I press my lips to your holy temples

and whisper, "I crash into things in the dark.

Even when the lights are on.

And I am wrong more often than I am writing,

and even them I am often wrong."

But when my friends are in the bathroom at the bar

rolling dollar bills into telescopes and claiming they can see god,

I will come to you open as my grandmother's bible,

and when you ask if I want to roll play alter boys

fucking in the church kitchen during Sunday mass

I will say, "Hell yes!

But only if you leave a hickey on my ass

in the shape of Jesus' palm.

So I can be sure I got nailed

down."

Heather, you will never loose me to the wind.

You are the lightning that made me fill my chest with candles.

You are the thunder clapping

for the poem nobody else wants to hear.

You are an icicle's tear

watering a tulip on the first day of spring.

You melt me alive.

You kiss me deep as my roots will reach.

And I want nothing more than to be an eyelash

fallen on your cheek,

a thing collected by your fingers

and held like a wish

I promise whatever I do

I will always try my best to come true.

TRELLIS

WITH THANKS TO J/J PLETHORA

There is a reason my body creaks like a closing casket
every time I fuck with the lights left on.

It is the same reason my friend sets fire to photographs of birds
and follows the smoke with pleading eyes.
We both had years when the phoenix didn't rise,
when we slept in beds of cindered feathers
and held hallow ashen beaks the way other kids held ice cream cones.
I sucked the bones of a songbird's charcoaled wing
and you think your pills are gonna fix me, doctor?
You think I'm gonna chase this down with water?
The shame as loud as his next girls nightmares?

I tied my tongue like a ribbon in my baby sister's hair,
like laces in the shoes of my little brother,
like a bow around a gift I gave to my father and mother,
and my silence equaled every Christmas morning
where we were still happy and grateful.
But my silence was also his next girl's eyes
falling like timber where no one chose to hear,

her roots ripped up,

her ground eroding to the din of an old man's zipper.

Twenty years later I wake in damp sheets

my body trembling to the ghost of her voice cracking like a frozen lake.

And I don't even knew her name.

Never saw her face.

Only heard the rumors

that he'd moved on to the hemorrhage of another perfect thing

And now here I sing through cinder,

through microphones raised like white flags in war zones,

through poems I've dug from my throat like fishing hooks.

From here I look back at my voice lowered to half mast.

How he must have stood there with his dirty hand on his dirty heart

laughing like a broken levy

as his next girl woke with body bags beneath her eyes

and enough shame in her gut to give the hurricane her own name.

If I could see her face, if I could face the I of her storm

how would I ever tell her that I speak for a living?

Would I offer my own wounds as condolence?

Would I tell her his claws carved me animal?

Would I say, "At fourteen years old I threw my bloody fists

into my boyfriend's face til his eyes swelled shut

and his tears turned crimson and his jaw cracked

til he cried so hard I was finally convinced his hands

were not every man's hands."

Would I tell her I have stood beneath street lamps

waiting for the swarming flies to identify my body as carcass,

to swallow every cell of salt

and leave nothing behind but the trellis

of my untouched bones?

I remember the fault lines in the corners of his eyes,

the way he shook hands with my father,

the smirk on his face beneath the swollen sun.

Even his shadow looked guilty.

The concrete made crime scene by its touch.

Would I tell her this?

Would I ask is she has ever outlined her own body with chalk?

"Is there yellow tape in your top dresser drawer

for those nights when your true love's touch is an anthem to a dead

    country

and you find yourself stumbling with rope burns around your neck

begging the bodies of strangers to not respect you in the morning?"

In the morning I shovel my blood from the white snow,

I wipe my frantic breath from the window,

and I bind my breasts so that something will hold my breath

so tight not even the air in my lungs could be identified as woman.

Woman,

Are you a carbon copy of myself?

Is there a boy inside you painting his cells

with the charcoal of cindered feathers

so he will never again glow in the dark the way girls do?

Woman,

if I knew your name,

If I could face the I of your storm

and the warning, locked in my voice box, that never came

would I tell you all of this?

And after that

would I ever find the nerve be to admit

that even if I could I would not take my silence back?

My father owned a gun.

He would have blown that man apart.

My mother owned a mother's heart.

Everything would have broken.

Everything but you.

BIRTHDAY

FOR JENN

At 12 years old I started bleeding with the moon

and beating up boys who dreamed of becoming astronauts.

I fought with my knuckles white at dust,

and left bruises the shape of Salem.

There are things we know by heart,

and things we don't.

At 13 my friend Jen tried to teach me how to blow rings of smoke.

I'd watch the nicotine rising from her lips like halos,

but I could never make dying beautiful.

The sky didn't fill with colors the night I convinced myself

veins are kite strings you can only cut free.

I suppose I love this life,

in spite of my clenched fist.

I open my palm and my lifelines look like branches from an Aspen tree,

and there are songbirds perched on the tips of my fingers,

and I wonder if Beethoven held his breath

the first time his fingers touched the keys

the same way a soldier holds his breath

the first time his finger clicks the trigger.

We all have different reasons for forgetting to breathe.

But my lungs remember

the day my mother took my hand and placed it on her belly

and told me the symphony beneath was my baby sister's heartbeat.

And I knew life would tremble

like the first tear on a prison guard's hardened cheek,

like a prayer on a dying man's lips,

like a vet holding a full bottle of whisky like an empty gun in a war zone...

just take me   just take me

Sometimes the scales themselves weigh far too much,

the heaviness of forever balancing blue sky with red blood.

We were all born on days when too many people died in terrible ways,

but you still have to call it a birthday.

You still have to fall for the prettiest girl on the playground at recess

and hope she knows you can hit a baseball

further than any boy in the whole third grade

and I've been running for home

through the windpipe of a man who sings

while his hands playing washboard with a spoon

on a street corner in New Orleans

where every boarded up window is still painted with the words

We're Coming Back

like a promise to the ocean

that we will always keep moving towards the music,

the way Basquiat slept in a cardboard box to be closer to the rain.

Beauty, catch me on your tongue.

Thunder, clap us open.

The pupils in our eyes were not born to hide beneath their desks.

Tonight lay us down to rest in the Arizona dessert,

then wake us washing the feet of pregnant women

who climbed across the border with their bellies aimed towards the sun.

I know a thousand things louder than a soldier's gun.

I know the heartbeat of his mother.

Don't cover your ears, Love.

Don't cover your ears, Life.

There is a boy writing poems in Central Park

and as he writes he moves

and his bones become the bars of Mandela's jail cell stretching apart,

and there are men playing chess in the December cold

who can't tell if the breath rising from the board

is their opponents or their own,

and there's a woman on the stairwell of the subway

swearing she can hear Niagara Falls from her rooftop in Brooklyn,

and I'm remembering how Niagara Falls is a city overrun

with strip malls and traffic and vendors

and one incredibly brave river that makes it all worth it.

Ya'll, I know this world is far from perfect.

I am not the type to mistake a streetlight for the moon.

I know our wounds are deep as the Atlantic.

But every ocean has a shoreline

and every shoreline has a tide

that is constantly returning

to wake the songbirds in our hands,

to wake the music in our bones,

to place one fearless kiss on the mouth of that brave river

that has to run through the center of our hearts

to find its way home.

FOR ELI

Eli came back from Iraq

and tattooed a teddy bear onto the inside of his wrist.

Above that a medic with an IV bag,

above that an angel

but Eli says the teddy bear won't live.

And I know I don't know but I say, "I know."

'Cause Eli's only twenty-four and I've never seen eyes

further away from childhood than his,

eyes old with a wisdom

he knows I'd rather not have.

Eli's mother traces a teddy bear onto the inside of my arm

and says, "Not all casualties come home in body bags."

And I swear,

I'd spend the rest of my life writing nothing

but the word light at the end of this tunnel

if I could find the fucking tunnel

I'd write nothing but white flags.

Somebody pray for the soldiers.

Somebody pray for what's lost.

Somebody pray for the mailbox

that holds the official letters

to the mothers, fathers,

sisters and little brothers

of Michael 19...Steven 21...John 33.

How ironic that their deaths sound like bible verses.

The hearse is parked in the halls of the high school

recruiting black, brown and poor

while anti-war activists outside Walter Reed Army Hospital

scream, "100, 000 slain,"

as an amputee on the third floor

breathes forget-me-nots onto the window pane.

But how can we forget what we never knew?

Our sky is so perfectly blue its repulsive.

Somebody tell me where god lives

'cause if god is truth god doesn't live here.

Our lies have seared the sun too hot to live by.

There are ghosts of kids who are still alive

touting M16s with trembling hands

while we dream ourselves stars on Survivor,

another missile sets fire to the face in the locket

of a mother who's son needed money for college

and she swears she can feel his photograph burn.

How many wars will it take us to learn

that only the dead return?

The rest remain forever caught between worlds of

shrapnel shatters body of three year old girl

to…

 welcome to McDonalds, can I take your order?

The mortar of sanity crumbling,

stumbling back home to a home that will never be home again.

Eli doesn't know if he can ever write a poem again.

One third of the homeless men in this country are veterans.

And we have the nerve to Support Our Troops

with pretty yellow ribbons

while giving nothing but dirty looks to their outstretched hands.

Tell me, what land of the free

sets free its eighteen year old kids into greedy war zones

hones them like missiles

then returns their bones in the middle of the night

so no one can see?

Each death swept beneath the carpet and hidden like dirt,

each life a promise we never kept.

Jeff Lucey came back from Iraq

and hung himself in his parents' basement with a garden hose.

The night before he died he spent forty five minutes on his fathers lap

rocking like a baby,

rocking like daddy, save me,

and don't think for a minute he too isn't collateral damage

in the mansions of Washington.

They are watching them burn and hoarding the water.

No senators' sons are being sent out to slaughter.

No president's daughters are licking ashes from their lips

or dreaming up ropes to wrap around their necks

in case they ever make it home alive.

Our eyes are closed, America.

There are souls in the boots of the soldiers, America.

Fuck your yellow ribbon.

You wanna support our troops,

bring them home,

and hold them tight when they get here.

POLE DANCER

She pole dances to gospel hymns.
Came out to her family in the middle of thanksgiving grace.
I knew she was trouble
two years before our first date.
But my heart was a Labrador retriever
with its head hung out the window of a car
tongue flapping in the wind on a highway going 95
whenever she walked by.

So I mastered the art of crochet.
and I crocheted her a winter scarf
and one night at the bar I gave it to her with a note
that said something like,
I hope this keeps your neck warm.
If it doesn't give me a call.

The key to finding love
is fucking up the pattern on purpose,
is skipping a stitch,
is leaving a tiny, tiny hole where the cold is
and hoping she fills it with your lips.

This morning I was counting her freckles.

She has five on the left side of her face, seven on the other

and I love her for every speck of trouble she is.

She's fricken awesome.

Like popcorn at a drive-in movie

that neither of us has any intention of watching.

Like Batman and Robin

in a pick-up-truck in the front row with the windows steamed up.

Like Pac man in the eighties,

she swallows my ghosts.

Slaps me on my dark side and says,

"Baby, this is the best day ever."

So I stop listening for the sound of the ocean

in the shells of bullets I hoped missed

to see there are white flags from the tips of her toes

to her tear ducts

and I can wear her halos as handcuffs

'cause I don't wanna be a witness to this life,

I wanna be charged and convicted,

ear lifted to her song like a bouquet of yes

because my heart is a parachute that has never opened in time and I wanna fuck up that pattern,

leave a hole where the cold is

and fill it everyday with her sun,

cause anyone who has ever sat in lotus for more than a few seconds

knows it takes a hell of lot more muscle to stay than to go.

And I want to grow

strong as the last patch of sage on a hillside

stretching towards the lightning.

God has always been an arsonist.

Heaven has always been on fire.

She is a butterfly knife bursting from a cocoon in my belly.

Love is a half moon hanging above Baghdad

promising to one day grow full,

to pull the tides through our dessert wounds

and fill every clip of empty shells with the ocean.

Already there is salt on my lips.

Lover, this is not just another poem.

This is my goddamn revolution.

I am done holding my tongue like a bible.

There is too much war in every verse of our silence.

We have all dug too many trenches away from ourselves.

This time I want to melt like a snowman in Georgia,

til my smile is a pile of rocks you can pick up
and skip across the lake of your doubts.

Trust me,

I have been practicing my ripple.

I have been breaking into mannequin factories
and pouring my pink heart into their white paint.

I have been painting the night sky upon the inside of doorframes
so only moonshine will fall on your head in the earthquake.

I have been collecting your whispers and your whiplash
and your half hour voice mail messages .

Lover, did you see the sunset tonight?

Did you see Neruda stretch out on the horizon?

Do you know it was his lover who painted him red?

Who made him stare down the bullet holes
in his countries heart?

I am not looking for roses.

I want to break like a fever.

I want to break like the Berlin Wall.

I want to break like the clouds
so we can see every fearless star,

how they never speak guardrail,

how they only say fall.

ROBBIE Q. TELFER

MENTAL GRAFFITI: ANOTHER CHICAGO POEM

Chicago, when will you be angelic?

When will you realize that the graffiti is a gift?

Perhaps when we realize that the hyper segregation you gave us is a
    gift too – a shitty one

You will never be resolved

Daily

you're defined & defied & defiled, sanctified

you're revised & reviled & revived, vandalized

you're revered & despised & derived, redesigned

you're reworked & reworn & reward, second prize

you always say that I'm fired before I say I've resigned

it's a sin when you shine, ecstasy when you die

through the din you're a joke that is dirty & divine

I miss you when I'm gone but ne'er do I pine

because no one pines anymore

and it's not your style

with all your scented floor cleaners, car air fresheners,

fake Christmas

trees

these are the only pines in your design

naturally unnatural, phallically vaginal, communal in your hermitude.

Words made for you hold you up

just as much as concrete and steel do

like a 3D dictionary in HD

    a mutually secret promise

    shared from us in the lispy spitting shush of color.

Shhhh (C)

We give you this gift

Shhhh (h)

We give you these words

Shhhh (i)

And I won't pitch a fit cuz you've been painting over our gifts

If you don't fetch the whip cuz I've been on the South Side

actually talking to black people.

See you in Hell

Sh(.)cago

AWKWARD SCARS

Do you see this one?

Got it from a sniper

Perched up by D'nang

See these?

Sharks – thousands of sharks

They came after me because I told 'em they were ugly sharks

This one's the shape of a lady

I got it from kissing the devil

In the manner of the French

The devil dared me to

And my pappy done told me:

"Boy, you always take on the devil's dares –

It's how you prove to God you ain't a faggot!"

I don't have a pappy who done tells me things…

Obviously

Our scars

Like accidental tattoos

Carry stories

That we tell

Whenever prompted

And because of the storyteller

And their personal brushes with varying degrees of danger

Each scar will inevitably reflect

Their keeper's personality

I knew a kid in high school

Who was cut across the stomach

By a bear while he was sleeping in a tent

He knew this made him a badass

And he acted like one too

Patrick

Has a keloid scar where they put in

One of those big metal bars

Through the cartilage in his ear

Because he asked them to do that to him

On purpose

Annie

Has a shimmering gash on her forearm

From when she fell into irony

Trying to play a prank

On her little sister

Each scar-bearer — badass, masochist, prankster —
Have their stock stories
They unfurl
Each time inquired about these
Individual imperfections
They are shamans of their skin
The storytellers of their flesh
Walking reminders of the pain
Their identity's culture has endured

Now I present for your consideration
My real scars
See if you can figure out who I am:

See:
On my left hand
A tiny slit from fourth grade 4-H carving class
My first and last 4-H carving class
I was trying to make a cowboy hat
Out of balsa wood and kept slipping
Kept cutting my hand
This scar is from when I was too
Embarrassed to ask for another band-aid

Because after my third
They started making fun of me

See:
Inside my right hand
A piece of pencil lead
It broke off when I jerked
My hand away from my
First and last 6th grade friend
Because he was trying to
Wipe his boogie on me

See:
About my face, chest, arms
Chicken pox craters
I started getting the little poxes
On vacation in Orlando
      My first and last
And I thought they were zits
So I kept aggressively popping them

See:
The back of my head
The roof of a bank

Blew off and landed on me

In the passenger seat of a Chevy Suburban

If I hadn't been slouching

I would have had my skull crushed

It was the first and last time

I've driven in a tornado watch

It was also the first and last time

A fucking bank landed on my head

See:

The bottom of my right foot

I stepped on a piece of glass

While running barefoot in the snow

For the first and last time

That was the joke!

Run barefoot in the snow!

I'm a fucking idiot!

See:

My right shin

I fell – slipped in wet paint

Playing paintball

For the first and second-to-last time –

I wanted to make sure paintball

Was fucking stupid
Turns out it is

That's all of them
All my inescapable stories
You probably have a good idea
Who I am now
But in those six little stories I've told
A thousand times
They've been edited
To fit tiny narrative arcs
Bite-size stanzas
So I can get through them
So I can represent just who I think I am
So I can pretend to control this pile of fear
I call Robbie Q. Telfer

But these aren't the stories
I wanna carry on my body
And they're not even the whole picture

See:
(left hand) carving class, never finishes or masters anything
(right palm) pencil lead, no genuine friendships

(face, chest, arms) chicken pox, always making things worse

(back of head) roof of bank, the sport of the Gods

(bottom of foot) broken glass, fucking stupid

(right shin)

    I didn't get the scar from paintball

    I got it from the doctors

    Who cut my leg open and drained it

    For an hour and a half

    Because I never healed from the paintball fall

    Internally

    And I was awake the whole operation

    And I was holding my mother's hand

    Crying

    While Greg, my step-dad, cracked jokes

    In the corner to keep me conscious

See:

(left hand) perpetual amateur

(right palm) friendless

(face, chest, arms) dumbass

(back of head) Godless

(bottom of foot) dumbass

(right shin)

And I know that Patrick and Annie and you

Have other scars too

With stories attached

That aren't and can't be

Perfectly resolved or publicly shared

If I could

I'd have excellent scars

Received as symbols for love lost

For those lost

That I need to be reminded of

The impact they've had on my skin

And it's expansion into this awkward man

That the landscape of my body is

Exactly what it is

Because of them

I want to be able to say,

"Oh, you see this canyon on my back?

That's my grandparents in the ground.

And see where half my face is missing?

That's Rick.

And see where the other half of my face is missing?

That's Greg."

How excellent. How accurate.

Have you seen this nature documentary?

It was on again recently

Where these beluga whales, dozens of 'em,

Get trapped in the arctic ice

Because winter freezes the sea around them

Before they can get out

So in order to survive the season

They have to continually surface for air

Just to keep a ten-foot

Hole in the ice from freezing over too

And they're surviving off stored blubber

Constantly looping

Dozens of 'em

Up and down from the surface

Now waiting at the opening

Is this polar bear

And she can see the belugas trapped

In their cycle of respiration

So the entire winter she dives in

On top of the whales

Digging deep into their beautiful

White, hydrodynamic backs

With her claws, with her teeth

Slicing them open

Permanently disrupting their

Perfect smooth innocence

Scarring them

And occasionally

Plucking them out like albino olives

She can eat a whole whale for days

Grimly she waits there

And the whales have to keep

Coming up for air

And she's waiting there

But they have to keep coming up for air

The bear she tears their

Backs but they keep coming back to it

I have to say, watching them die

Makes me a little enraged

I understand why they don't just give up

But only in that way that acceptance becomes

It's own kind of understanding

The ones who survive

Get to swim away

But not as fast

Not without their

Hydrodynamic backs

No longer intact

The bear is fat

From their thinned pack

And scarred ruined backs

Their beautiful, perfect backs

The story

The life

The beluga's back

All perfect in theory

And my scars, my stupid stories

I'm stuck with them

The mirror's speakers bleat to me daily

Remember remember remember

They have to keep coming up for air

I'm pressing the delete key

Erasing the tales that fill the holes

Where my skin used to be

See:

(left hand) this is my grandparents in the ground now

(right palm) this is Stacy, my friend

(face, chest, arms) this is you, my friends

(back of head) this is Rick, my brother

(bottom of foot) this is for me, because I'm a fucking idiot sometimes,
    and I shouldn't forget that fact

(right shin) this is Greg, my other father, half of my face

Stories are deceptions

But if we tell the right ones

Progress is possible

I'm only sorry my scars are not excellent

The story

The life

The beluga's back

I promise more awkward accidents

I promise more loss

There will be pieces of me

Buried and burned

Scraped and scorned

They're reserved for you

Because winter always comes

And she's up there

And she's hungry too

Counter-intuitively we will keep

Returning to her for air

Because we know, we remember what

The water feels like

Rushing through us

While our symphony of muscles

Sings us forward

Hot bullets shot haphazard about

Those warm summer seas, the seas

Swirling and tickling the cracks and crannies

In our almost perfect skin

We remember and we will remember

What that feels like

And we want it again and again forever and again

Go back and taunt the bear with your being

Go back with your backs to her

Sing your underwater stories to her,

You ghosts

You shamans

You canaries of the sea

Do it for Pappy!

Return

Return

Delete

Return

You will taste excellent

Return to her

For the first time

For the last time

CONCRETE JUNGLE

Zoom in, take the picture:
There's a fenced-in field of grass I pass
everyday somewhere near the very center
of Chicago
And despite this field being comprised
of cinder blocks, busted bricks, Sarajevo-level debris
the grass decides to grow here anyway.

Obviously, we're the grass
Despite the discrimination, segregation, gentrification
despite the Truth we all go die
despite the truth that writing about struggle is cliché
despite all this
we grow, we live, we write anyway.
Symbolically, we're the grass.
Clearly.

But let's talk about the non-
symbolic field for a moment.
The actual grass that sprouts here emerges
un-metaphorically fuzzy,

like the whole thing is out-of-focus

distinct urban debris punctuates this fluctuating static

sea of yellow-green.

And that's beautiful.

Not beautiful because only I hold the poetic keys to beauty

Not beautiful because mother nature is stronger than humanity

No – sometimes shit is pretty.

Why does everything have to *mean* something?

I love this fuzzy fenced-in field and

I want to turn the poet off when I see it.

It's neat.

I like it.

It makes me smile.

The wind pets it like a dog raised to old age with love.

It waves at me like an almost forgotten

flashbulb memory that I haven't judged yet.

Zoom in, take the picture:

I'm a little kid,

chin on knees,

leaning against a garage now torn down absently

pulling on the limbs of an action figure

peering in at the darkness inside its organless carapace.

Zoom out

in the 20 years since that snapshot

I've learned to clutch onto all and any

anxiety-free serenity.

I know it's only temporary

I know the real sadness this field of grass holds and represents

I know what grows on graves

I know this

I don't ever stop to frolic, skip

work or abandon responsibility

but if you don't occasionally

collect these small soundless images,

meditations of secular reverence,

an invisible nihilistic selfish shell will

grow slow from your inside out

until you completely forget why

man invented cameras in the first place.

Zoom in:

There's a broken red pick-up truck in my mother's

driveway that belongs to a dead man.

Weeds patiently burst from the hood and sun-bleached bed.

Bees dance and zoom out of the now quiet engine block.

So much depends on the red pick-up truck beside a torn down garage.

I love the dead man, I hate that truck

I love the weeds, I love the bees, I love the yellow-green grass.

Now you try. Take the picture.

ROCK, ROCK, ROCK 'N' ROLL HIGH SCHOOL

Right before I was born,

I went to High School at the top of the Washington Monument.

This was the late 70s,

back when you either understood punk rock instantly

or you didn't,

and scaling the sleek walls of that capital donger every morning

was more than a hassle in a leather jacket.

The pigeon shit up there got thick,

but punk and

high school and

the 70s

were all about moving so fast you couldn't assess

damage or disco or whose fuck you was louder –

the state to the world or

you to the state

of the world.

I don't think any of us even had other fingers,

just big hard cocks shooting out the center of our pale knuckles,

fuck you fuck you fuck you!

All my teachers were too coked out and harried to mark me late,

being pretty was illegal,

my cold shell was half sweat half freedom,

we all failed and graduated anyway.

Our smiles were stinking sneers,

we wore our gym clothes in the snow

obliterating nature with attitude,

Carter left the keys to his dick in his other pants.

For my science project, I punched my buddy in the mouth

his blood was my book report.

Black and white skeletons

esoteric Luddites

pikes through our pussies, out our screaming faces

electric pomp and

similar circumstance.

1980, I was born.

The partitioned cafeteria persists.

THE IGGY POP HORROR SHOW

The main character
in the slasher flick
but he's no heroine.
Too beautiful and addled
too slutty experienced to spare.

Every night he's murdered
invisibly while the Stooges
amplify baby death rattles,
the crowd scream-laughing
as he gets what he deserves.
Final Girl, speedy shell-less
turtle, unstoppable meaty steel
in a peanut brittle world.

Prepping for the horror
he shoots up gallons of blood
to refill his chest's armored tank
to splatter and awe
to open the spigot
let the motherfuckers drown.

YOU CAN'T SPELL FUTILITY WITHOUT UTILITY

Although he'd sewn sleeves into Earth
he felt more like ass than Atlas
with his arms underground
air-dangling legs like that
it's hard to get a foothold on sky
it's hard to wear your world
when it's constantly wearing you
upside
down.

Can I ask you a question?
Thanks. (that was the question)

He, you, whatever
continues to peddle
at nothing
trying for a chunk of real
to be flown by
(from Oz monkeys with strict orders)
so he can plant toe
invert heaven cycle

get the blood to vacate

sad strained forehead veins

get down to the business of

economical shrugging

the center of everything

get down to getting

gravity's tugging hugging

his clothes, his skin

worn, lovely, breathless

the center of everything.

In the meanwhile he's missed

the advertising projected

on the full moon's face

though necessity requires

that he piss on his own –

face and necessities –

inadvertent expert he's

destiny's momentum jacket he's

dysfunctional finger worming at

the center of everything.

Who's to say there's a winner

in the war of us vs. the dust?

Thanks. (that was the question)

CRISTIN O'KEEFE APTOWICZ

WARRANTEE

We are not responsible

for any omissions or inaccuracies found here

for the validity of these posting

for any damage this may cause

We are not responsible

for anyone trying these stunts

for anyone not reading the directions fully

for anyone's beliefs beside my own

We are not responsible

for your actions

for our actions

for anything our salesmen promise or state during the sale

We are not responsible

for lost luggage

for lost messages

for damaged goods

We are not responsible

for losses that are incurred by you

for anything that may happen to you

for seagulls eating your funnel cake

We are not responsible

for any injury or damage you may have caused yourself

for any injury or damage you may be causing yourself

for any injury or damage that may occur in the future

We are not responsible

for anyone, but ourselves

We are not responsible

for the whole world, you know

We are not responsible

for the past so we are not

saying we're sorry

SALUTATORIANS

Never on the soccer field,
our shoulder blades pressed
into the hot buggy dirt.

Never in the backwoods
our eyes and fingers wet,
hair caught in our mouths.

Not in the back row
of the theatre, the backseat
of the car, not in the closet

while our brothers cleared
the table. Nope, not us.
We never turned up

a radio, never turned down
a light, never tucked a bra
into a coat pocket, a condom

into an envelope, never left

halfway through a prom,

never had a pregnancy scare.

Never had to have the talk,

never had to apologize

to her parents, to your parents.

Never had to get looks

from teachers, from students,

in fact, never got looks.

What did we get? Pats

on the back, straight As,

driver's licenses the day

we turned sixteen. We got

extra credit, anxiety disorders,

letters of recommendations

from our rabbis. We got

summer jobs, we got

unpaid internships, we got

scholarships to colleges

our parents otherwise
wouldn't be able to afford.

They told us we were having
"real life experiences," said
we were preparing ourselves

in ways that our peers weren't,
and I wish I could say we'd
have traded it all in for the heat,

for the magic, the all that young
stickiness, but the truth was we
liked it clean, liked it quiet.

Each heavy book in our bag
a brick, a stepping stone,
a non-refundable ticket out.

FOR THE PEOPLE AT BOOKSTORE READINGS WHO KEEP ASKING ME WHY I STILL SLAM NOW THAT I HAVE "REAL BOOKS" OUT

Because the microphone slouches like bad boy
whose neck I want to choke.

Because sometimes the poem punches its way
off my tongue, and other times it needs to be
dragged out by my ribcage by its hair.

Because I have said things in front
of a roomful of strangers that I would never
say to my own mother and for good reason.

Because I have heard poets say things
in front of roomful of strangers that made me
pulse, made me sweat, made me want to push
further, risk everything, be that beautiful.

Because sometimes I have felt that beautiful.

Because sometimes I have felt ugly too

and it was okay.

Because I still have stories to tell.

Because I have had my heart broken.

Because I have had my heart broken and survived.

Because I have had my heart broken, survived
and someone told me the poem I wrote about it sucked.

Because I survived that too.

Because the bear hugs, because the *uh-huhs*,
because of the venomous looks people give
to the guy whose cellphone starts ringing.
Fuck you, Asshole! Can't you see
we are listening to poetry here!

Because people are listening to poetry here.

Because there is poetry here, every cracked voice,
every stutter, every stumble is poetry. Every
shaky piece of paper held by shaky hands,

every nervous laugh, every awkward pause: poetry.

Every braided head, every untied shoelace,

every spilled beer, every *Yo, this is first time*

I'm doing this, every *Man, it's been a minute,*

it's feels good to be back, every time the poet

says, *This is some new shit* and people

in the audience lean forward like a dare,

like they are looking for a light,

and the poet's flint be sparking.

Because some nights I didn't feel like it
and it seemed like those were the nights
I needed it the most.

Because I've won, and it didn't make me
more of poet.

Because I've lost, and it didn't make me
less of poet.

Because I've cheered until my throat ran raw,
laughed and cried and fell on the damn floor
like fool, for poetry.

Because I am a fool for the poetry.

Because of the poetry.

Because this is poetry.

AT NIGHT ON TOUR

Albany is so quiet
I mistake the cat
for a burglar.
The keyboard sounds
like a kettle drum.

Apparently everyone
we know in Chicago
lives in a 3rd floor
walk-up yet we never
meet a single neighbor.

In San Francisco,
I look for food
in the dark, find
19 boxes of tea
and jar of seeds.

In Vancouver,
there isn't any
toilet paper.

For three days:
stolen napkins,
paper towels,
wadded receipts.

In Texas,
the shaggy red dog
knows the minute
you wake up, chases
away the thumb-sized
junebugs skittering
in the bathroom.

In Nebraska,
I eat leftovers
from breakfast out
of styrofoam,
as the TV advertises
the state fair,
a crops report,
no joke, a sitcom
about church.

In Vermont,

good-looking single
platonic friend sleeps
on the cot. We both
say goodnight,
hearts pounding:
Go to sleep! Go to sleep!
The radiator kicks in.

In Melbourne,
I take your shirt
out of the ziplock bag
just to huff it, it didn't
smell like you, until
suddenly it did.

In L.A.,
I'm half-afraid to wake up,
chatted out, project-barren,
New York-lusty, New York-lonely
remembering the final straw,
a neon sign: Hollywood Bagels

THE CHARMLESS STARLING

I read a poem about a starling
and thought, *I want to write a poem
about a starling*, an inelegant starling,
a charmless starling clattering its way
across my city's staggering blue sky.

Then I remember: I don't think I've ever
seen a starling. In fact, my foggy uncertain
vision of them is largely based on tattoos,
which I'm not even convinced are starlings.
They could be hummingbirds or blackbirds,

or even trustworthy boring old sparrows
for all I know. In a drawing class once,
the teacher asked that we all draw a chicken,
well, draw a chicken from memory, and
I drew a nice, round chicken teapot,

without realizing at all what I was doing.
I'd never seen a live chicken, or at least,
one that wasn't crammed into a wire cage

on the backs of trucks, stacked, really,

not unlike teapots. Funny, I always thought

I had a fairly rural upbringing, but that

was mostly because I lived in Philadelphia

and not New York City. Compared to

New York City, everything can seem a little

provincial. My first week in New York City,

and the RA in our dorm asked us all

to talk about our favorite animals and list

the traits we loved about them. Afterwards,

the RA announced it was a test, a psycho-

logical test, that the traits we admitted to

liking about our favorite animals were

really traits we liked about ourselves.

We all felt a bit tricked, a bit exposed.

I immediately regretted my choice. Why

did I announce my love of the platypus,

its webbed feet and leathery bill, its ability

to lay eggs but still nurse its young with

warm lapped milk, the fact that scientists

have studied the platypus for years and

still don't know what the hell to make of it

SONYA RENEE TAYLOR

COMMUNION OF GLASS

A preparation like communion or confession
Ritual carved into the enamel of teeth
Brush them
Shine the wig
Squeeze the last drop
Out of the gloss
Or into the girdle

Breathe

After this, breaths are shorter
A vice calibrating my rib cage
Reminding me of the myriad of ways I shrink myself
Knelt over the tub scrubbing the sole of a dirty shoe
The bulimia of a woman to lazy and vain to vomit
All in efforts to spit shine a photograph
Some days I regret having ever taken

There is this
A broken red light in my throat
And the next word is still waiting for the light change

For the glue to dry on this cheap vase

I cracked trying to sell to you

Mute is not always silent

And breaking into splinters

makes it easier to give yourself away

I am a communion of glass

I do this not in remembrance of me

I do this as forgetting rounds the edges

Makes me less likely to bleed as the shards go down

After all

Wouldn't want to ruin this pretty dress

It is the only thing

Holding me together

FRAGILITY OF EGGS

Once when baking a cake
in clumsy haste
I dropped an entire carton of eggs on the floor
the twelve infant orbs lept from the styrofoam container like
tiny suicide bombers colliding with the linoleum
in a slow motion waltz of misfortune

I had just seconds before the
impending calamity
taken one loose egg
out of fridge and placed him
on the counter
Karma kissed
he became the lone survivor of his clan
escaping the splattered fate of a dozen others
the only egg undamaged

My gradmother was 1/4 fire tongued gypsy
1/4 sugary cake baking lady and all the rest
Alcoholic
Snapping peas and knee caps with lightning ferocity

she kept close company with the fifth of vodka tucked in her bed

having years before evicted grandad to the nearby lazyboy recliner

Round with frail little coffee stirrers for legs

she made me laugh jaw clenched hearty

like grandmothers should do

with witticisms and a discourse bluer

than a richard pryor stand up routine

grandma was a marvel of a mess

the kind of mess that happens when

clumsy people don't handle fragile things

delicately

She bore thirteen children

to an angry man who tongue kissed her

with iron shovels

and a cement heart

8 boys and 5 girls

handsome and pretty and unlucky

The number thirteen seems to call misery

like a drunken ex-lover at 3am

so it was no surprise when the phone rang

Ike her 5th eldest boy

a 20 year old miscreant in the midst of a misdemeanor

shot

twice through the heart

splattered on the sidewalk of a neighbors home

the first useless yolk

Richard the 4th eldest boy

loved white women in the 1970's

in a way that left only one thing certain

about the rape charges

He would serve the full 25

Calvin Jr 2nd boy

the one that made all the folks on the block

say, "Irene girl, you spit him out!

Ain't a bit of big calvin in em."

caught the backwash of her vodka at twelve and sipped

until his liver looked just like his daddy's fist

Lani the 2nd eldest girl

followed suit

Gerald

schizophrenic

Joyce bipolar major depressive

Ronnie, Raymond, Danny, Gary

Edna, Terry

all inhaled ten dollar diamonds until

lost babies and anonymous blow jobs filled

their fractured ribcages

Shaved their bones thin as shells

A dozen cracked lives

The final egg avoided the slippery hands of

fate for so long

Grandma believed she'd actually saved her

Just one

Perhaps plucked from the carton seconds before

the violent collision of poverty, blackness

and dreams pressed so tight

that the pulp bleeds right out of them

spilled her like the rest

Ruthie

the only one to finish high school

the "She doing good for herself" girl

All us offspring of the tortured twelve

looked on in admiration

Whispered bout our auntie.

Dressed to the 9's

None of us really understood the anatomy of an egg

How the fondle of filthy fingers

thins the porous skin of it

How misleading is the notion of

Solid

Leave little indication that the inside

of an egg may have long been dead

But sometimes God

In all his gorgeous backbiting mercy

spares us the open hand smack

of arrogance

So it was

Grandma

bald, blind and filled with cancer

died before she would have to witness

Ruthie stuff the forty dollar rent money

she trusted only her to pay

inside her empty spaces

and let the crack man begin to excavate

until the Sheriff pad locked the doors

and placed 8 decades of whatever

we could salvage and the shells of 13 eggs

on a project curb for the vultures to pick

Grandma is a decade old memory now but

I wish I could tell her I smelled vanilla

on my mothers breath on her 7 year clean anniversary

The oven seems to always be heating

when I visit my now sober aunt Ruthie.

She tells me she has started baking again

Uses grandma's recipes

I ask her how they've been turning out (the cakes)

She says she hasn't quite gotten it yet

as she takes the eggs from the fridge

and places them on the counter

without the slightest quiver of hand.

I smile

wink at a shadow in the corner with coffee stirrer legs

and tell her,

this time she will.

SILENT

Listen Laugh,

Dance Sing

Watch

We Laugh

Listen

    Dance

        Sing

            Watch

We watch

We sing

We dance

We laugh

We listen

But never asked Miles

What Kind of Blue

makes a magic music man wrap his fingers

around the neck of something that ain't

a trumpet?

Is it the kind of black blue

Cicely Tyson might have turned when

134

He choked her
When the air inside her finally
Halted and hiccupped
like a scratched copy
of Bitches Brew?

Is it a kind of blue tarnish
that settles over your manhood
when you fear she might out shine
your pretty polished horn
so you beat her
till she's a dull shade of cobalt

It doesn't matter
cuz we listen
dance sing watch

Laugh

when Rick James told us,
"Cocaine is a hell of a drug"
Would we have
Stomach stitches
Doubled over

if producers asked

Frances Alley

The woman he tied and gagged

to be on T.V.

Show us how skin

buckles like tin foil

when you place a sizzling

crack pipe against it

Chuckle loudly

at the rope burns

Vaginal lacerations

from his multiple rapes

Could she

host the BET Awards?

While we

Laugh Listen Sing Watch

Dance

Like a little bastard girl for an R&B singer

In a puddle of our own urine

Will we give her millions?

Make her R. Kelly triple platinum

Sell out concerts

to hear her tells us

how she mounted him and wondered

if maybe he looked

like the daddy she ain't ever met

of course we will

dancelaughlistenwatch

Sing

"It's A Man's World"

Know he reminded his wives

He was Black and Proud

With fist and fury

To jaw, hip, eye

Nose, throat

We sang with James

Felt unified but not enough

To speak

Challenge

Ask

Help

Her/Him

We just sang

It is easier when

they black our eyes

The Perfect excuse not to see

How we sing dance listen laugh

Watch

Wesley's movies

Swoon

Finally exhaled

At the chocolate movie star

On the screen

Blamed Halle

For being dumb enough

to let some man pummel

Her pretty little face

Beat her eardrum

to a tiny pulp of useless flesh

Deafen her to the sound

of her own screams

While we watch listen laugh

dance sing

so somebody tell Cicely

she wasn't worth it

Tell cord bound kidnapped Frances

we would rather

Be entertained

Tell our fifteen year old

Daughter

To let him piss on you

if the album is at least gold

Or wait until we can

hold their corpses in our palms

Kill all the psalms written to useless

Women who's backalley bedroom

Barely audible screams

disrupt

the next movie scene

So yes,

Sing dance listen watch laugh

Laugh watch dance sing listen

Listen laugh dance sing watch

Watch

Watch

Watch

or

will

We speak

ON ASPIRATIONS
(LACI PETERSON RESPONDS)

"I'ma go to college and find a nice boy and get married. A few years later, we'll have babies. Momma says you should spend a little time alone with your husband because babies change everything."

— 9 year old girl's answer to what she wants to be when she grows up Phipps Mall, Atlanta, GA

Pretty little girl child,
They call it Coffin Birth.
The way the gases in my bloated womb
expelled Conner into the marina water
like a bottle uncorked
Tethered by a rotted umbilical cord
Death does not quell desire
nor does it staunch longing
Never have I wanted to cradle
To cleave to anything
As desperately as my son
Floating just beyond my grasp

The first gulp of harbor water stung less

Than Scott's infidelities

Less than the first phone call from

The first "her" he would parade past me

His new trinkets

So many trinkets followed that by the end

I had become quite adept at the art

of swallowing the hard to swallow

By then it was a simple task

Letting the tide

fill my lungs

Constrict me out of my flesh

We were plastic perfect

A prosthetic matrimony

A stock photograph

Taken in front of the remodeled kitchen counter tops

Where he would mount other women when

I went shopping

A dutiful and consummate homemaker

A good wife

Who does not ask too many questions

So when he put me in the car

I went without a fight

Now this is my legacy
News articles chronicling the only thing
I ever did that mattered to this world
Die
Sopping and decayed
Washed ashore without any arms
To hold my baby boy

Yes love

Babies change everything
They make you want
to impart wisdom greater than casserole recipes
And how to scramble his eggs just so
They make you want more
Than their daddies fractured affections
Dream bigger than perfect drapes
And multi karat engagement rings

Babies change careless fucks
Into double homicides
Candle light vigils

And search parties

Scouring nearby roadsides

for where he might have dumped our bodies

Child I give to you what

I can no longer have

Identity

Your own precious self

Materialized into what ever audacious

Request you may make to this universe

Fantasy so outlandish

It must BE

Aspirations beyond

Any he you may love

And yes, the sweet and tender kiss

The holy presence of life in your belly

Is a wondrous gift

But sometimes our selfish imaginings

The kernel we keep for ourselves

May be the only difference

between life and death

So be careful sweet

Choose your dreams cautiously

Never forget

All I ever wanted to
Be
Was Scott's wife

ON REMEMBRANCE
("THE FALLING MAN" WIDOW SPEAKS)

My knees still buckle like the south tower

when our youngest daughter

Not old enough to remember

But ripe enough for wondering

Asks about her daddy?

"Tell me again momma!" she says

and I stitch a blanket of explosive heroism for this child

a story perfect enough

For silver screens and morning talk shows

Write her father into unmerited glory

It is a tale of blooming mushroom clouds of confetti in heaven

for a father who endeavored to lead others

past the orchestra of snapping metal beams

but died in exodus

As unblemished as an American flag

This lie is prettier than truth

It is a pretty she can carry to school yards

fully intact

The truth

she would have to scrape off the sidewalk

Wait like her mother for the building to collapse

so she might receive the consolation of a free

110 story headstone

scripting his epitaph in the ash of concrete

At night after she has been tucked into sleep

Underneath this magic quilt

I am left to ponder in the dark

Photograph in hand

if his was an exit of valor

Was it the equivalent of a slave's propulsion

into iced Atlantic waters

Defiant against the fate of bondage

or was it something else

How long before that day had he eyed the air

outside the 73rd floor like a mistress's ass

Waiting for an anonymous moment to touch it

Maybe he had always planned to leave with her

Bone-weary of bills and the worry in my kiss

Nauseous of the smell of milk on his daughter's breath

Was he ready to leave and here was his moment

I have been cheated out of the catch
No panties left carelessly in the car
No smell of burning sulfur on his collar that morning
Just questions

He was a building on fire
Leaving me to write the front page story
All about his leap from flames
From us

There is no pretty in this
Thus I will lie
Because anything is prettier than telling her
That daddy became a dodo bird
Awkward, flightless and extinct

Only begetting layman archaeologists
Who will dig up his bones every September
Study them and wonder
Why he did not try to survive

AUTHORS' WEBSITES

Derrick Brown: brownpoetry.com

Andrea Gibson: andreagibson.org

Buddy Wakefield: buddywakefield.com

Anis Mojgani- myspace.com/anismojgani

Robbie Q. Telfer: myspace.com/theenvironment

Cristin O'Keefe Aptowicz: aptowicz.com

Sonya Renee: myspace.com/sonyareneeisreal

OTHER GREAT WRITE BLOODY BOOKS

THE LAST AMERICAN VALENTINE: ILLUSTRATED POEMS TO SEDUCE AND DESTROY
24 authors, 12 illustrators team up for a collection of non-sappy love poetry
Edited by Derrick Brown

SOLOMON SPARROWS ELECTRIC WHALE REVIVAL
Poetry Compilation
by Buddy Wakefield, Anis Mojgani, Derrick Brown, Dan Leamen & Mike McGee

I LOVE YOU IS BACK
Poetry compilation (2004-2006)
by Derrick Brown

BORN IN THE YEAR OF THE BUTTERFLY KNIFE
Poetry anthology, 1994-2004
by Derrick Brown

DON'T SMELL THE FLOSS
New Short Fiction Pieces
by Matty Byloos

THE CONSTANT VELOCITY OF TRAINS
New Poetry
by Lea Deschenes

HEAVY LEAD BIRDSONG
New Poems
by Ryler Dustin

UNCONTROLLED EXPERIMENTS IN FREEDOM
New Poems
by Brian Ellis

LETTING MYSELF GO
Bizarre God Comedy & Wild Prose
by Buzzy Enniss

CITY OF INSOMNIA
New Poetry
by Victor D. Infante

JUNGLESCENE: UNDERGROUND DANCING IN LOS ANGELES
A sweaty modern photographic historical journey
by Danny Johnson

WHAT IT IS, WHAT IT IS
Graphic Art Prose Concept book
by Maust of Cold War Kids and author Paul Maziar

MISS BLISS AND THE LOST RED NIGHT
New Poems
by Mindy Nettifee

NO MORE POEMS ABOUT THE MOON
NON-Moon Poems
by Michael Roberts

CAST YOUR EYES LIKE RIVERSTONES INTO THE EXQUISITE DARK
New Poems
by Danny Sherrard

LIVE FOR A LIVING
New Poetry compilation
by Buddy Wakefield

SOME THEY CAN'T CONTAIN
Classic Poetry compilation
by Buddy Wakefield

WRITEBLOODY
QUALITY AMERICAN BOOKS AND PRINTING

PULL YOUR BOOKS UP BY THEIR BOOTSTRAPS

Write Bloody Publishing distributes and promotes great books of fiction, poetry and art every year. We are an independent press dedicated to quality literature and book design, with offices in LA, NYC and Murfreesboro, TN.

Our employees are authors and artists so we call ourselves a family. Our design team comes from all over America: modern painters, photographers and rock album designers create book covers we're proud to be judged by.

We publish and promote 8-12 tour-savvy authors per year. We are grass-roots, D.I.Y., bootstrap believers. Pull up a good book and join the family. Support independent authors, artists and presses.

Visit us online:

WRITEBLOODY.COM

Printed in the United States
127769LV00001B/61-129/P